Ready-Ed Publications

Solving Maths Problems For Lower Primary

By Anita Green

Title: Solving Maths Problems For Lower Primary
© 2016 Ready-Ed Publications
Printed in Ireland
Author: Anita Green
Illustrators: Terry Allen, Alison Mutton

Acknowledgements

i. Clip art images have been obtained from Microsoft Design Gallery Live and are used under the terms of the End User License Agreement for Microsoft Word 2000. Please refer to www.microsoft.com/permission.

Published by:

Ready-Ed Publications
PO Box 276 Greenwood WA 6024
www.readyed.net
info@readyed.com.au

ISBN: 978 186397 969 6

Contents

Teachers' Notes

This book contains a series of open-ended maths problems based on fun and engaging stories. The problems are placed into real life everyday contexts in which the students are likely to find themselves. It's important for students to know that open-ended maths problems have more than one answer and that students often need to add to the information to be able to solve them. For example, if the problem is: 'If I have 30 tablets, how many days will it take me to finish them all?', students need to decide how many tablets the patient is required to take each day, to work out how many days it would take to finish the course. They could work out answers for 1 a day, 2 a day, 3 a day, etc.

A benefit of using open-ended problems is that all students in one class, with their range of experiences and mathematical knowledge and skills, can be working on the same problem. This is because these problems can be solved using a variety of strategies, which means students can tackle them at their own level.

You will notice that the problems based on the stories have accompanying support and extension questions. This allows for further differentiation. If there are students who seem to be struggling with the main problem (this will often happen when you are first introducing these kinds of problems) it is a good idea to have a support question on hand for them to attempt first. In my experience usually once students have worked through the support question they are then ready to move on to the main question. The extension questions are there for the students who solve the main problems quickly to challenge them further.

Reflection time is important when implementing these lessons, not just at the end of a lesson, but also during it. It is important to stop at regular intervals and share how students are tackling the problems. This allows students to share successes and to learn about a range of different strategies. It also helps those students who may be struggling or are using a strategy that isn't working for them.

The questions that you pose during these lessons are also important. These questions can help students delve deeper or think more critically. For example:

- What would happen if…?
- Can you do it a different way?
- How do you know….?
- Have you found all the answers?
- How could you make this problem more challenging/easier? (This question encourages them to take responsibility for their own learning.)
- Prove it! Convince me!
- Can you show me/explain to me how you got your answer?
- Can you find a pattern?

This book will help to address Reasoning as students are required to show and explain their thinking and working out. Understanding may also be shown as students need to have some understanding of mathematical concepts taught, to be able to apply the knowledge to solve a problem.

Ready-Ed Publications

Section One:
At The Park

AT THE PARK

SUPPORT & EXTENSION QUESTIONS

1. What do you think is the number of the first house in Chelsea's street? What do you think is the number of the last house in Chelsea's street? How many houses do you think are in the street altogether?
   Support: If there are just 10 houses in the street and the numbers go up in twos, what might the pattern be?
   Extension: What is the pattern? Can you create a different pattern for the letterbox numbers?

2. What might the temperature have been yesterday and what might it be today?
   Support: What if the difference is just 3 degrees?
   Extension: Tomorrow is going to be 13 degrees warmer than yesterday. What might the temperature be tomorrow?

3. How do you get to your closest park? Can you draw a map and show the path that you take?
   Support: Draw a map of your local park. What sort of play equipment is there?
   Extension: Write out a set of directions that someone could use to get to your local park.

4. How many ants do you think Chelsea can see?
   Support: How many legs are there on 3 ants?
   Extension: Can you work out how many legs there are on 8 ants?

5. Draw what the pattern might look like.
   Support: What might the colour pattern be if there are red, blue and yellow beads?
   Extension: Create three different patterns. Give your most difficult pattern to a friend and see if they can complete it.

6. How many beads might be in each group and how many beads is this altogether?
   Support: If there are 12 beads altogether, how many are there in each group?
   Extension: Can you find all the numbers from 20 to 40 that can be divided into 3 equal groups?

7. How many legs do you think there might be?
   Support: How many legs are there on 5 dogs?
   Extension: At first Chelsea counted 46 legs, but she knew that couldn't be right. How does she know that she wasn't right?

Ready-Ed Publications

AT THE PARK

SUPPORT & EXTENSION QUESTIONS

8. How many conkers might Chelsea have in each pile?
Support: If there are 12 conkers in the first pile, how many are there in the second pile?
Extension: How many different answers are there? Can you find a pattern?

9. What coins might they be and how much might they total?
Support: How much money might Chelsea have if the coins are all gold?
Extension: If the coins are all different, what is the most and least amount of money Chelsea could have?

10. What time might Chelsea and her Dad have arrived at the park and what time might it be now that they are leaving?
Support: If they arrived at 1.15pm, what time would it be when they left?
Extension: Chelsea and her Dad had actually only been at the park for 1 hour and 45 minutes (not quite 2 hours). What time might they have got there and what time is it now that they are leaving?

Discussion (before):

- ❑ Do you have a park near your house?
- ❑ Can you walk to it?
- ❑ Do you have a favourite park?
- ❑ What do you like about it?
- ❑ What sort of equipment do parks normally have?
- ❑ What do you like to play on at the park?
- ❑ What do you do at the park?

Discussion (after):

- ❑ What is your house number?
- ❑ What is the pattern of house numbers in your street?
- ❑ Can you put the house numbers into a different pattern?
- ❑ Take a photograph of your school's playground. Can you find different shapes?
- ❑ If I have 20 stones and I collected them during three separate trips, how many might I have collected during each trip?

Ready-Ed Publications

A MATHS STORY - AT THE PARK

Read the story *At The Park* and solve the problems along the way.

Dad and I decided to walk to the park. As we walked past the houses in our street I read out the numbers on the letterboxes, "24, ……26, ……28, ……30, ……32."

34!

"What number do you think will come next Chelsea?" Dad asked before we reached the next house. I thought about this. The numbers on the letterboxes were in a pattern. "34!" I said. As we strolled down the street I thought about the numbers on the letterboxes.

1. What do you think is the number of the first house in Chelsea's street? What do you think is the number of the last house in Chelsea's street? How many houses do you think are in the street altogether?

Chelsea's Street

The weather was unseasonably warm! The difference between the temperature yesterday and the temperature today was 7 degrees!

2. What might the temperature have been yesterday and what might it be today?

Temperature	
Today	**Yesterday**

Ready-Ed Publications

It was a bit of a walk to get to our closest park. We turned left out of our house, took the next right and then the third left and the park was at the end of that street.

3. How do you get to your closest park? Can you draw a map and show the path that you take?

Your House

Your Local Park

When we finally arrived at the park, I ran straight to the slide and climbed up the steps. I slid down on my belly! As I hit the bottom of the slide I saw a row of ants climbing over a sweet wrapper. I could see more than 20 little legs!

4. How many ants do you think Chelsea can see?

As I headed over to the swings, I passed counting beads attached to a long horizontal pole. The counting beads were all different shapes and colours. The beads made shape and colour patterns.

5. Draw what the pattern might look like.

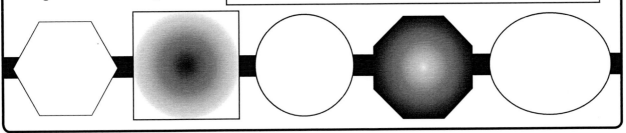

I pushed the beads all the way to the other side of the pole. Then I slid them back again. Then I moved some along the pole so they were in 3 equal groups.

6. How many beads might be in each group and how many beads is this altogether?

While swinging as high as I could on the swings, I watched as two people walked by each holding a bunch of leads. There were big dogs, small dogs, black dogs, brown dogs, short-haired dogs and long-haired dogs!

7. How many legs do you think there might be?

Next, I headed to the sandpit and decided to build something. I remembered that there were heaps of conkers along the tree line at the back of the park so I went to collect some to use in the sandpit. I collected as many as I could fit in my jacket and took them to the sandpit and then went back for a second pile. In the two piles, I had 30 conkers altogether.

8. How many conkers might Chelsea have in each pile?

Ready-Ed Publications

I decided that I needed more items for my creation. I went to get some stones from a pile near the swings. While rifling through the stones I found three coins buried underneath them.

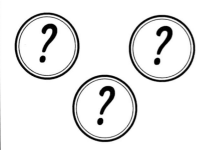

9. What coins might they be and how much might they total?

 "Time to go Chelsea!" Dad called.

"Already?" I complained.

"We have been here for 2 whole hours!" Dad explained. Wow, that had gone fast. I wondered what the time was.

10. What time might Chelsea and her Dad have arrived at the park and what time might it be now that they are leaving?

I love visiting different parks. This one would have to be my idea of the perfect park – it was a great design.

Activity 1 - Design A Park

Parks and playgrounds can have lots of different pieces of equipment that are made up of many different shapes.

❑ Design your own park below using as many different shapes as you can. You might like to give your park a name.

❑ How many different shapes did you create in your park? List the shapes below and write how many of each shape you created.

Shape	How many?

Ready-Ed Publications

Activity 2 - Piles Of Stones

❏ At the park Chelsea collected a pile of stones that she was going to use to section off a patch of ground for her toys. She collected 30 stones in total but she collected them in two separate trips. How many might she have got on her first trip and how many might she have collected on her second trip?

Using a 20-sided dice, roll it to find out how many stones she collected on the first trip and then work out how many she must have collected on her second trip.

First trip (roll the dice)	Second trip

Variations

❏ Change the number. Make it 50 stones altogether. Or 27 stones.

❏ Roll two 10-sided dice and add the number together first.

❏ Imagine that Chelsea collected the 30 stones in three trips. How many might she have collected each time?

Section Two:
Shopping Trip

Ready-Ed
Publications

SHOPPING TRIP

SUPPORT & EXTENSION QUESTIONS

1. What might the coins be that Matt's Mum pays with?
    Support: If one of the coins is a €2 coin, what might the other coins be?
    Extension: What if there are 7 coins altogether? What if there are 10 coins altogether?

2. What might the 3 coins be that the butcher hands back to Matt's Mum?
    Support: If all three coins are the same, how much might the coins total?
    Extension: How much money does Matt's Mum get back? What is the least and the most change that she could receive from the butcher?

3. How many other ways could Matt's Mum have paid for the card?
    Support: Can you find coins to make exactly €3.95?
    Extension: Can you find three different ways to pay €3.95? Can you work out the change that Matt's Mum might get back?

4. What date might Uncle Dave's birthday be on and what date might Charlie's birthday be on?
    Support: If Uncle Dave's birthday is on August 20th, when is Charlie's birthday?
    Extension: What is the earliest date that Uncle Dave's birthday could fall on? What is the latest date that Charlie's birthday could fall on?

5. How long do you think that it will take Matt to save €59.95 for the skateboard?
    Support: If Matt saves €10 a week, how many weeks will it take him to save up enough money to buy the skateboard?
    Extension: If it takes 10 weeks for Matt to save the money, how much will he have to save each week? What if Matt saves €7.50 a week - how long will it take him to save up enough money to buy the skateboard?

6. What might this pattern look like?
    Support: If the pattern is in 2s, what might it look like?
    Extension: If the price of each book is in Euro and cent, what could the pattern be? Make 3 different patterns.

7. What might the time be now and at what time do Matt and his Mum need to pick Matt's sister Charlie up?
    Support: If it is 3 o'clock now, what time do they need to pick Charlie up?
    Extension: What if Matt and his Mum still have an hour and 15 minutes before they need to pick Charlie up - what might the time be now?

8. How many toffee apples might be in the array?
    Support: If there are 3 toffee apples in each row, how many might there be in the array? Draw what this might look like.
    Extension: How many different arrays can you make? Can you find a pattern?

SHOPPING TRIP

SUPPORT & EXTENSION QUESTIONS

9. How many people could Matt share 24 chocolate bars with?
   Support: What if he shared just 12 chocolate bars? How many people could he share them with evenly?
   Extension: What if he had 30 chocolate bars? How many people could he share them with evenly?

10. What might the original prices of the DVDs have been and what might the DVDs be priced at now?
    Support: If the original price of a DVD was €10, how much does Matt have to pay for a DVD in this store?
    Extension: What if the saving was only a quarter off the original price?

Answers

Discussion (after) (Page 16)
If I have 5 coins in my purse. What might they be and how much do I have?
E.g. 5 x €1 = €5
2 x €2 plus 2 x €1 plus 1 x 50c = €6.50
1 x €1 plus 1 x 20c plus 3 x 5c = €1.35

I have 3 friends and I want to share some sweets with them. How many sweets do I need if I want to share them equally?
E.g. 30 sweets will give them 10 sweets each
15 sweets will give them 5 sweets each
24 sweets will give them 8 sweets each

Activity Pages
Money Amounts (Page 21)
E.g. 2 x €2 plus 1 x 50c plus 1 x 20c plus 1 x 10c plus 1 x 5c
3 x €1 plus 3 x 50c plus 3 x 10c plus 1 x 5c

Saving Money (Page 22)
E.g. €2 a week = 19 weeks. €4 a week = 10 weeks. €5 a week = 8 weeks.
€3.50 a week = 11 weeks.

Piggy Bank (Page 23)
Matt has €7.75 in his piggy bank.

Discussion (before):
- Do you go shopping with Mum or Dad or other family members? What do you shop for?
- Do you pay for items when you go shopping?
- Do you have your own money?
- How do you get your money? Where do you keep it?
- What do you do with your money?
- Where does money come from?

Discussion (after):
- I have 5 coins in my purse. What might they be and how much do I have?
- Can you work out how long it is between your birthday and a friend's birthday?
- I have 3 friends and I want to share some sweets with them. How many sweets do I need if I want to share them equally?
- Can you create a pattern with money? See if a friend can continue this pattern.

A MATHS STORY: SHOPPING TRIP

Read the story *Shopping Trip* and solve the problems along the way.

"Ok what's on the list?" asked Mum. I had a look. "First on the list is bread," I told her. So we headed to the bakery.
"That will be €2.65," the lady said. I watched as mum pulled out the exact amount of coins from her purse and handed them over.

1. What might the coins be that Matt's Mum pays with?

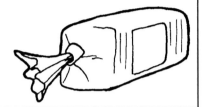

"Sausages next," I told Mum, and we headed to the butchers.
"Can we please have 8 sausages?" Mum asked the butcher. He handed over the sausages as Mum gave him a €5 note. The butcher handed 3 coins back to Mum.

2. What might the 3 coins be that the butcher hands back to Matt's Mum?

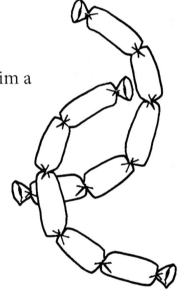

"What else do we need?" asked Mum "We need a birthday card and wrapping paper," I knew this was for Uncle Dave's birthday on the weekend. So we headed to the newsagents. Mum let me choose the card (it was so funny!) and then she handed over two €2 coins to pay for the €3.95 card.

3. How many other ways could Matt's Mum have paid for the card?

I can't wait until Uncle Dave opens his card. I hope that he finds it as funny as I do! His birthday is in August and my sister Charlie's birthday is in September. There is only 16 days between their birthdays.

4. What date might Uncle Dave's birthday be on and what date might Charlie's birthday be on?

Uncle Dave

Charlie

Mum and I headed into another store to get something that Mum had just thought of that wasn't on the list. While she was browsing through some things I noticed a skateboard on display. There were pictures on the box of a boy doing some amazing tricks! "Can I get this?" I asked, knowing that I had no hope.

"For €59.95!" exclaimed Mum. "No, you will have to save up your pocket money for that I'm afraid."

5. How long do you think that it will take Matt to save €59.95 for the skateboard?

Can I get this?

For €59.95!

Ready-Ed Publications

As we were leaving the store I noticed a row of picture story books on a shelf, that were on sale. I noticed that the prices on the tags made a pattern.

6. What might this pattern look like?

"What time is it?" asked Mum. I checked my watch and told her. "We better hurry. We have to pick your sister up in 45 minutes."

7. What might the time be now and at what time do Matt and his Mum need to pick Matt's sister Charlie up?

"Fruit shop next," I told mum. While Mum loaded a basket with apples, pears, strawberries and more, I was eyeing off the toffee apples. They looked delicious! They had been arranged in an array that made a perfect square.

8. How many toffee apples might be in the array?

Mum handed over a note to pay for all her fruit. I looked across at the sweet shop and saw that they were selling bags of 24 chocolate bars for only €6. I thought that sounded like a pretty good price.

9. How many people could Matt share 24 chocolate bars with?

"I think that's it!" Mum said. "Let's go." On the way out of the shops I noticed an advertisement for DVDs that were half price. What a bargain!

10. What might the original prices of the DVDs have been and what might the DVDs be priced at now?

50% OFF!

The prices of our DVDs have been slashed to half price!

As we hopped in the car, I decided that I was going to go home and count my money in my money box. Then I was going to come up with a list of ways that I could earn more money to save up for that skateboard. I had a big, blue pig and I knew it was at least half full. I wonder how much money was in it….

How much money is in your money box?

Wash the car, weed the garden …

Ready-Ed Publications

Activity 1 - Money Amounts

There are many different combinations of notes and coins that you can use to make any amount of money. How many different ways can you make €4.85? Can you draw 4 different ways below? How many coins have you used each time?

Which way above would you most likely pay €4.85 and why?

_____

_____

_____

Activity 2 - Saving Money

❑ Matt really wants to save up €38 and purchase 2 new DVDs that he saw at the shops. He gets pocket money, so he is trying to work out how long it will take him to save for these DVDs. Can you work it out for him using different amounts each time?

Amount saved per week	Working out	How many weeks it will take Matt to save
€2		19 weeks

Ready-Ed Publications

Activity 3 - Piggy Bank

❏ Can you work out how much money Matt has in his piggy bank? Count the coins below.

€

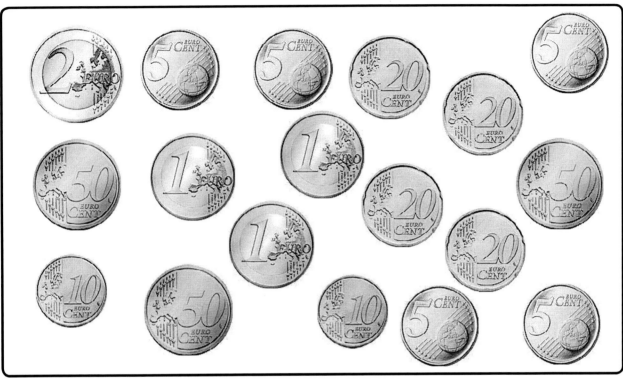

❏ Explain two ways that you could add up all this money.

Method 1: _____

Method 2: _____

❏ Highlight the most efficient method.

❏ How could you teach someone else how to add it up quickly?

_____

❏ Create your own piggy bank. Grab a small handful of coins and record what you have. Add up the coins and record the total.

Coins in my piggy bank	Total

Section Three:
In The Garden

IN THE GARDEN

SUPPORT & EXTENSION QUESTIONS

1. What might the pattern of flowers look like on the deck?
   Support: Can you draw what the flowers on the deck might look like if there are 3 different types of flowers?
   Extension: What might the pattern look like if there are 5 different types of flowers?

2. How many plants might be in the garden? What might the array look like?
   Support: Can you draw what the array might look like if there are 5 plants in each row?
   Extension: How many different arrays can you make for between 30 and 50 plants?

3. How many spots might be on each wing?
   Support: If there are 9 spots on its left wing, how many spots are there on its right wing?
   Extension: What if there are 33 spots on the ladybird's wings in total?

4. How many spots might this ladybird have altogether?
   Support: If there are 6 spots on one wing, how many spots are there altogether?
   Extension: What if one wing has double the amount of spots than the other wing? How many spots might there be in total?

5. What shape might the garden bed be? Can you draw what it might look like?
   Support: What if the garden bed was another shape with 4 sides? What might it look like?
   Extension: How many different shapes could the garden bed be?

6. How tall might Nicole's sunflower have been before, and how tall is it now?
   Support: If the sunflower was only 3 centimetres last week, how tall is it now?
   Extension: If the sunflower grows 2 centimetres a day for two weeks, how tall would it be after two weeks? What if it grows 2.5 centimetres a day?

7. Can you draw what Nicole's graph might look like?
   Support: What if the first measurement that Nicole recorded was 2 centimetres and the sunflower is now 20 centimetres tall?
   Extension: Can you create two different types of graphs using the same information?

8. If Nicole places three seeds in each hole, how many seeds would she need altogether?
   Support: What if Nicole has 9 holes to fill?
   Extension: If the holes are spaced out so there are 5 centimetres between each hole, how much room does she need?

IN THE GARDEN

SUPPORT & EXTENSION QUESTIONS

9. How many legs do you think Nicole sees altogether?
   Support: If there are 5 spiders, how many legs does she see?
   Extension: If Nicole counts 56 legs, how many spiders are there?

10. How many seeds do you think could be in the tomato?
    Support: If Nicole cuts the tomato in half and counts 15 seeds on one side, how many seeds do you think are in the tomato altogether?
    Extension: What if the answer is an odd number with a 3 in it? How many different answers could there be?

Answers

Activity Pages
How Many Legs?
Page 32

Ants	Spiders	How many legs
0	6	48
1	5	46
2	4	44
3	3	42
4	2	40
5	1	38
6	0	36

Discussion (before):

- Do you have a garden at your house? Who looks after it?
- What can be in a garden?
- What's in your garden?
- What do you need to do to look after a garden?
- How long does it take plants to grow?
- Have you ever planted anything yourself?
- What creatures might you find in a garden?

Discussion (after):

- Draw a pattern of flowers. Think about the colours as well as the number of petals.
- Plant a sunflower. Estimate its growth and find a way to record regular measurements. Later you can graph the results.
- When is the best time of year to plant seeds? Work out a time for planting and then work out when the plant will be fully grown (or ready for picking if it is a vegetable).
- Design a garden for an area in your school. Think about the shapes of the garden beds, how the plants will be arranged and any paths that you might need. Where would be the best place for your garden? Think about how much sunshine each area gets.

Ready-Ed Publications

A MATHS STORY: IN THE GARDEN

Read the story *In The Garden* and solve the problems along the way.

I picked a pink flower from our garden, held it to my nose and took a deep breath in. I had to admit the smell from the mix of flowers in the garden was amazing.

I continued to pick flowers and then lay them out on the deck in a pattern. I was going to make a bouquet for Aunty Jess for her birthday. I picked the flowers in a particular order.

1. What might the pattern of flowers look like on the deck?

After I had taken the flowers inside and had made the bouquet, I decided to check the vegetable garden and see how the tomatoes were going. Dad and I had put the garden together a year ago. We had planted all the vegetables in an array.

2. How many plants might be in the garden? What might the array look like?

As I was checking out the lettuces I noticed a couple of little ladybirds. I noticed that the first one had 17 spots on it in total.

3. How many spots might be on each wing?

Then I noticed the second ladybird was a little different. This one had the same number of spots on each wing.

4. How many spots might this ladybird have altogether?

Dad and I had recently built another small garden bed. All our other garden beds were square shaped or rectangular but this one was a different shape.

5. What shape might the garden bed be? Can you draw what it might look like?

I went to check on our sunflowers. My brother Stuart and I had planted sunflowers and had been measuring them regularly and recording the results. I grabbed the measuring tape and read the number where the top of my sunflower was sitting. Wow! My sunflower had grown 8 centimetres in the last two weeks!

6. How tall might Nicole's sunflower have been before, and how tall is it now?

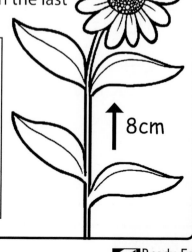

8cm

Ready-Ed Publications

Grown much?

8cm!

Dad came out into the garden just as I had finished measuring the sunflower. "Grown much Nicole?" he asked. "8 centimetres!" I exclaimed. He was amazed! He handed me the clipboard that we use to record the results and some blank paper. "Maybe you should graph your results so far," he suggested.

Not a bad idea. I had a look at the results. This was the second really big difference since I had started measuring the sunflower. There were two other times when there had been no or very little difference in the sunflower's height.

7. Can you draw what Nicole's graph might look like?

"When you're done over there come and help me plant some more seeds," said Dad. When I headed over to Dad he had made a line in our new garden bed and had two packets of seeds in his hand. He had made a small hole at the start of the line and dropped three seeds in. "Can you make holes like this every 5 centimetres and drop three seeds in?" asked Dad. Sounded easy!

8. If Nicole places three seeds in each hole, how many seeds would she need altogether?

As I put the last of the seeds in, I noticed a trail of baby spiders climbing up the outside of the garden bed. I wondered if there was a big mummy or daddy spider nearby!

9. How many legs do you think Nicole sees altogether?

"I'm making a salad for dinner!" Mum yelled out the window. "Can you pick me some cherry tomatoes please?" We went to pick some tomatoes for Mum. Dad held up a rather big cherry tomato. "How many seeds do you think are in this tomato?" he asked. I began to use all my powers of estimation to help me to try to work this out.

I'm making a salad for dinner!

10. How many seeds do you think could be in the tomato?

We cut the tomato open and started counting. "Do you think there is exactly that many seeds in every cherry tomato?" Dad asked. Hmmm… I wasn't sure. It was a big tomato, did that mean it would have more seeds?

What do you think? How many seeds would the average cherry tomato have?

Ready-Ed Publications

Activity 1 - Vegetable Garden

❑ Nicole has just built a big square garden bed to plant her vegetables in. How many plants do you think she can fit in? How many plants could be in each row? Can you draw 4 different ways below that her plants could be arranged?

1.	2.
3.	4.

❑ Nicole builds another garden bed for some flowers that she wants to grow. She has 30 flowers to fit in there. Can you show how she could plant these flowers below?

❑ Can you draw another way that she can plant these flowers on the back of the sheet?

Ready-Ed
Publications

Activity 2 - How Many Legs?

❑ There are many different creatures that live in gardens. Two creatures that live in gardens are ants and spiders. If there are 6 ants and spiders altogether in a garden, how many ants might there be and how many spiders might there be? How many legs would you see altogether? Fill in the table below showing how many ways you could make up these 6 creatures in total and how many legs there would be.

Ants	Spiders	How many legs?
0 ants = 0 legs	6 spiders = 48 legs	0 legs + 48 legs = 48 legs

Variations

● Increase the amount of creatures.

● Change the animals, for example, to cats and birds.

● Pair up. Each student rolls a 6-sided dice to work out how many creatures there are. The first to work out how many legs there are, wins.

 Ready-Ed Publications

Activity 3 - Sunflower Graph

❏ We often use graphs to record data that we have collected. Below is some data that has been plotted on a graph. It shows how much a sunflower has grown. Can you complete the graph?

Title: _____

Height

x

x   x

x

x

x

x   x

x

Days

❏ Can you complete the table to show the above information in the graph?

Day	Height

Ready-Ed
Publications

Section Four:
The Easter Egg Hunt

Ready-Ed
Publications

THE EASTER EGG HUNT

SUPPORT & EXTENSION QUESTIONS

1. Did Kai's Uncle and Aunty really hide a million eggs? How many eggs do you think they might have hidden? Roughly how many does this mean each child might get?

   Support: What if Kai's Uncle and Aunty have hidden 30 eggs?

   Extension: How many eggs do you think it will take to fill all of the children's baskets?

2. Can you draw what the 3 eggs might have looked like?

   Support: What if they are all pink, blue and yellow?

   Extension: What if there are 5 colours on each egg?

3. Can you draw what the eggs might look like?

   Support: What if there are just 12 eggs altogether?

   Extension: What if one quarter are pink and the rest are green? Can you draw what this might look like?

4. How many footprints do you think there are if the path of footprints matches the length of Kai?

   Support: Trace around your foot and cut it out. Use it to find out how many footprints long you are.

   Extension: Estimate how many footprints long your room is. Or how many footprints long is the distance from your classroom door to the toilets.

5. What might this egg look like?

   Support: Can you create a design on one half of the egg and give it to a friend to complete so that the egg's pattern is completely symmetrical?

   Extension: What if the egg has 2 lines of symmetry?

6. If the egg has the same amount of spots on each side, how many spots might there be on each side? How many spots might there be on the egg altogether?

   Support: What if there are 7 spots on one side?

   Extension: If there are 36 spots altogether, how many spots are on each side? How did you work this out? How would you explain your working out to someone else?

7. What time might the children have started hunting and what time might it be now?

   Support: If the children started hunting at 3.30pm, what's the time now?

   Extension: If there is 20 minutes left until the end of the hunt, what time will the hunt finish?

THE EASTER EGG HUNT

SUPPORT & EXTENSION QUESTIONS

8. If Mia's basket isn't half full, how many eggs might she have? Kai's cousin Zac's basket is overflowing. How many eggs might he have?
    Support: If Mia has 16 eggs and her basket is half full how many eggs might she have if her basket is less than half full?
    Extension: How many eggs might Mia and Zac have altogether, if they combine their baskets?

9. Can you work out how many eggs Mia might have?
    Support: Use a hundreds chart. How many even numbers are there with a 4 in it?
    Extension: What if the number is even or odd? How many different numbers could it be now?

10. How many eggs might we each have?
    Support: If Kai has 23 eggs, how many eggs does Ayla have?
    Extension: What if Kai has 3 times as many eggs as Ayla? How many might they each have?

Answers

Discussion (after) (Page 36)
If a group of children have a pile of eggs at the end of an Easter egg hunt, how might they be shared evenly? How many eggs might each child receive?
E.g. 5 children and 20 eggs = 4 eggs each
3 children and 24 eggs = 8 eggs each
10 children and 100 eggs = 10 eggs each

Discussion (before):

❑ Do you celebrate Easter?
❑ What sort of traditions do you and your family follow at Easter?
❑ Have you ever taken part in an Easter egg hunt?
❑ Have you ever taken part in a scavenger hunt of any kind?
❑ Who do you celebrate Easter with?
❑ Where do you celebrate?
❑ Do you go away for Easter?
❑ How much chocolate do you get at Easter?
❑ How long does your chocolate last?

Discussion (after):

❑ How many eggs do you think you would need to have a successful Easter egg hunt?
❑ How many eggs would each person get on an Easter egg hunt?
❑ Many Easter eggs have symmetrical patterns. Where else can you find something that is symmetrical?
❑ Can you find something symmetrical at your school?
❑ Can you draw a picture or pattern that is symmetrical?
❑ If a group of children have a pile of eggs at the end of an Easter egg hunt, how might they be shared evenly? How many eggs might each child receive?

Ready-Ed Publications

A MATHS STORY: THE EASTER EGG HUNT

Read the story *The Easter Egg Hunt* and solve the problems along the way.

"On your marks … get set … GO!" I ran and grabbed the three little eggs that I had my eye on at the edge of the garden bed. It was the annual Easter egg hunt at Uncle Les' and Aunty Theresa's house. Every year we had a delicious Easter breakfast feast followed by an Easter egg hunt. They would hide what seemed like a million eggs and give me, my sister and each of my four cousins a basket each which we would then go and fill!

1. Did Kai's Uncle and Aunty really hide a million eggs? How many eggs do you think they might have hidden? Roughly how many does this mean each child might get?

I went around to the back of the house and found three more eggs under the clothesline. The eggs all had the same three colours on their wrappers. Each egg, however, had its own individual pattern.

2. Can you draw what the three eggs might have looked like?

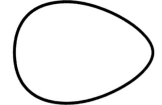 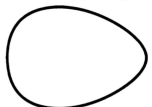 

I moved around to the other side of the house and found a group of little eggs. I wasn't even sure they had been hidden. It looked like they had just been left there and forgotten about. Half of them were green and half were pink.

3. Can you draw what the eggs might look like?

I threw the eggs in my basket and headed into the front garden to see how many I could find there. I could see the Easter Bunny's footprints leading up to the front door. I think the path of prints was as long as me!

4. How many footprints do you think there are if the path of footprints matches the length of Kai?

The first egg that I spotted in the front garden was sitting in a low branch of a tree all by itself. It was a decent sized egg and had the most colourful outer wrapping that I had ever seen. The patterns were perfectly symmetrical!

5. What might this egg look like?

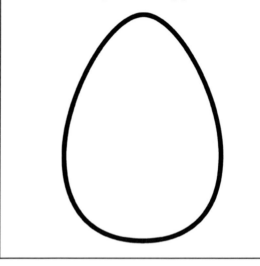

I saw my cousin Zac out the corner of my eye heading through the side gate. I quickly scanned the garden to see how many eggs I could find. I reached out to grab a spotted egg underneath the letterbox. It was orange with white spots on one side and with black spots on the other.

6. If the egg has the same amount of spots on each side, how many spots might there be on each side? How many spots might there be on the egg altogether?

It felt like we had been hunting for eggs for ages! When I checked my watch I was surprised to see that we had only been hunting for half an hour.

7. What time might the children have started hunting and what time might it be now?

As I continued to hunt, I collected 5 more medium-sized eggs, one large egg, 15 little solid eggs and 2 cream eggs. My basket was over half full! As I was eating one of my eggs, Mia and Zac raced passed me.

8. If Mia's basket isn't half full, how many eggs might she have? Kai's cousin Zac's basket is overflowing! How many eggs might he have?

Ok, it was time to get serious. I looked up. Already I could see a few eggs on the top rung of the fence and one more in the peg basket near the clothes line. I ran around and grabbed as many eggs as I could find. I was amazed at how many I had missed first time around.

"Ok I think that's it!" Aunty Theresa called us all back in to the house. We sat down to count our eggs. "How many do you have?" I asked Mia once she had finished counting.

"It is an even number with a 4 in it," she announced.

9. Can you work out how many eggs Mia might have?

At the end of a hunt, we share our eggs and always make sure that everyone has a similar amount. In the end there was only a difference of 9 eggs between my basket and my sister's basket.

10. How many eggs might we each have?

Another successful Easter egg hunt! We thanked Uncle Les and Aunty Theresa for all our eggs. "Don't eat them all today," joked Uncle Les. Today?! Surely that wasn't even possible! I wondered how long it would take me to eat the whole basket. Could I make my eggs last until next year's Easter egg hunt?

Ready-Ed Publications

Activity 1 - Easter Egg Designs

❑ Easter egg wrappers have lots of different patterns on them. Use the first egg shape below to design your own Easter egg pattern.

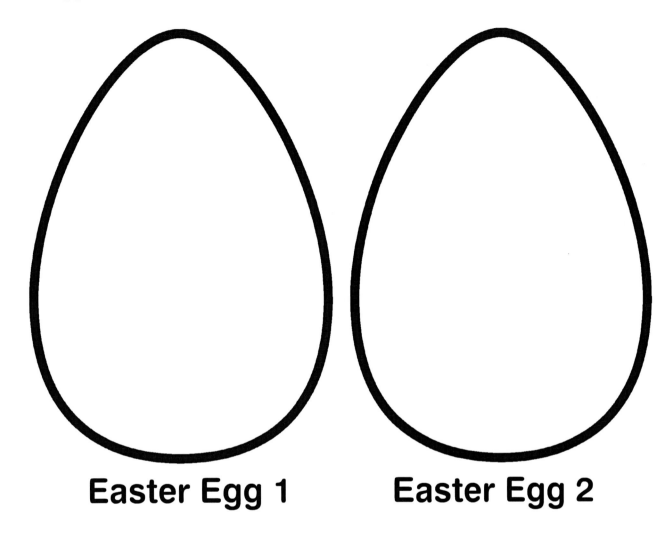

Easter Egg 1   Easter Egg 2

2. See if you can describe the pattern that you have created on the first Easter egg to a friend. Can your friend create this pattern from your description?

3. Next, ask your friend to describe the pattern that he/she has created to you. See if you can draw it on the second egg above.

4. Does your pattern match your friend's pattern? Why/why not?

_____

_____

5. Is your pattern symmetrical? Can you make one with a symmetrical pattern on the back of this page?

 Ready-Ed
Publications

Activity 2 - Easter Egg Plans

❑ Imagine that you have to hide some eggs around the school yard for your friends to find. Where would be the best hiding places? Draw a map of your school yard and mark where you would hide 20 eggs. Create a key for your map below.

The Treasure Map

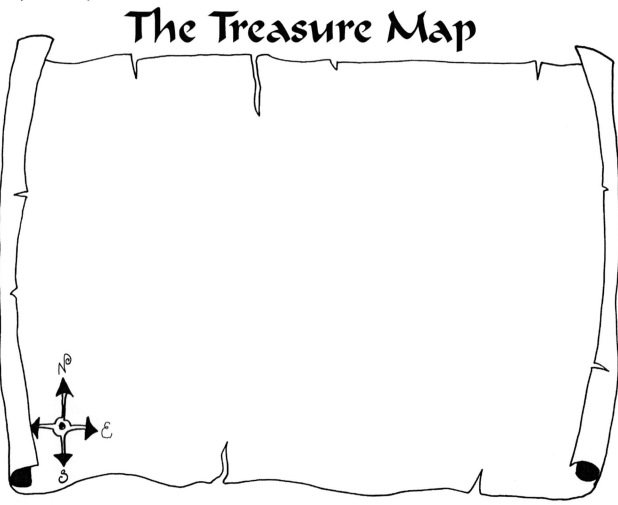

Key

	easter egg		

Ready-Ed Publications

Activity 3 - How Many Eggs?

How many Easter eggs you find during an Easter egg hunt compared to others, could be down to just plain luck rather than skill.

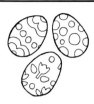

❑ In this game you and your partner take turns to roll the dice to find out how many eggs you find. The player with the most eggs after 6 rolls is the winner!

Player 1		Player 2	
Number rolled	Total eggs	Number rolled	Total eggs

1. Who won this game?

_____

2. How much by?

_____

Variations

● Change the dice – 6-sided, 10-sided, 20-sided.

● First to get to a target number - 20 (or 50 or 100).

● Add a new rule – even numbers you add on, odd numbers you take away.

Section Five:
On The Farm

Ready-Ed
Publications

ON THE FARM

SUPPORT & EXTENSION QUESTIONS

1. How many 6-egg cartons might be needed for all the eggs in the bucket?
   Support: How many 6-egg cartons would be needed for 24 eggs?
   Extension: What if there are 12-egg or 24-egg cartons?

2. Dad said the temperature was going to be 11 degrees higher than it was yesterday. What might the temperature have been yesterday and what might it be today?
   Support: What if the difference in temperature is only 5 degrees?
   Extension: What if the difference in temperature is 19 degrees?

3. If Justin and Bailey collect one more egg each day than the previous day, how many eggs would they have by the end of the week?
   Support: If they only collect one egg on the first day, how many eggs would they have by the end of the week?
   Extension: What if they collect two more eggs each day than the previous day? What if they collect 3 more eggs each day than the previous day?

4. How many chickens might be in each coop?
   Support: If there are 12 chickens in one coop, how many are there in the other coop? What if there are only 2 more chickens in one coop than the other?
   Extension: What if there is a third coop with 13 more chickens in than the first coop? How many chickens are there altogether?

5. Bailey counts 30 legs when looking at the pigs and the geese. How many pigs and geese might there be?
   Support: If there are 9 geese, how many pigs would there be?
   Extension: Have you found all the answers? What if there were 42 legs?

6. What might the containers look like?
   Support: Can you draw 3 different looking containers that you think would all hold the same amounts of water?
   Extension: Can you find 3 different looking containers that you think would hold similar amounts of water? Estimate how much each container would hold and then measure to find out the exact amount.

7. Bailey counts 25 animals in the paddocks. How many horses might there be and how many cows might there be?
   Support: If there are 10 horses, how many cows are there?
   Extension: How many different possibilities are there?

8. What time might it be now and what time might Bailey have got up?
   Support: If it is 11 o'clock now and the chime goes every hour, what time did Bailey get up?
   Extension: What if the cuckoo sounds every half-hour instead of every hour?

ON THE FARM

SUPPORT & EXTENSION QUESTIONS

9. How many pieces might be needed altogether?

Support: If Bailey is setting the table for 4 people, how many pieces are needed?

Extension: Can you think of any other items that might be needed on the table? How many pieces will this be in total?

10. If Nan sells the jam for €2 a jar, how much money will she make?

Support: If Nan sells 5 jars, how much money will she make? What if she sells 10 jars of jam?

Extension: What if Nan drops the price to €1.50 per jar of jam?

Answers

Discussion (after) (Page 46)

If there are 30 sheep in 2 paddocks, how many might be in each paddock?
E.g. 17 and 13 or 12 and 18 or 9 and 21
How many 6-egg cartons are needed to hold 16 eggs?
3 cartons (leaving 2 empty spots)
What about to hold 42 eggs?
7 cartons

Activity Pages
Earning Money (Page 52)

	Amount Given	Total
Day 1	€1	€1
Day 2	€2	€3
Day 3	€3	€6
Day 4	€4	€10
Day 5	€5	€15
Day 6	€6	€21
Day 7	€7	€28
Day 8	€8	€36
Day 9	€9	€45
Day 10	€10	€55

How Many Legs? (Page 53)

Horses	Ducks	Sheep
2	16	2
4	10	3
6	6	3
2	2	9
5	12	1
1	18	2

Discussion (before):

❑ Have you ever been to a farm?
❑ Do you know anyone who lives on a farm?
❑ What animals live on farms?
❑ What's your favourite farm animal?
❑ What jobs need to be done each day on a farm?
❑ Have you ever been to a market?
❑ Have you or your family ever sold anything at a market?

Discussion (after):

❑ If there are 30 sheep in 2 paddocks, how many might be in each paddock?
❑ Find two containers - one should look like it holds twice as much as the other container. How can you work out if you're right?
❑ If you wake up but don't get dressed until half an hour later, what time did you get up and what time did you get dressed?
❑ How many 6-egg cartons are needed to hold 16 eggs? What about to hold 42 eggs?

Ready-Ed Publications

A MATHS STORY: ON THE FARM

Read the story *On The Farm* and solve the problems along the way.

"Cockadoodledooooooooooooooo!" I sat up and rubbed my eyes. "What time is it?" I mumbled.

"Welcome to life on the farm!" smiled Dad as I walked very sleepily into the kitchen. It was school holidays and we had come to stay with Nan and Pop for a week on their farm.

Dad was cooking breakfast and he had a bucket of eggs on the counter. I wondered if they had been collected this morning. Next to the bucket was a stack of egg cartons each designed to hold six eggs.

1. How many 6-egg cartons might be needed for all the eggs in the bucket?

"Breakfast is going to be a little while so do you want to go and get dressed?" Dad asked. "It's going to be a warm one today, so dress light."

2. Dad said the temperature was going to be 11 degrees higher than it was yesterday. What might the temperature have been yesterday and what might it be today?

In turned out that those eggs weren't collected today. After breakfast Pop asked if Justin and I wanted to go and collect the eggs. So we got our boots on and headed down to the chicken coop. We got quite a few more eggs to add to the bucket.

3. If Justin and Bailey collect one more egg each day than the previous day, how many eggs would they have by the end of the week?

Ready-Ed Publications

Before we left the chicken coup, we had to feed the chickens. They seemed really hungry! There were two chicken coops side-by-side. Although they were the same size, I noticed that there were 8 more chickens in one coop than the other.

4. How many chickens might be in each coop?

On our way to feed the horses we passed the pigs and the geese. There were little piglets running around. I knew that Justin would want to take one home!

5. Bailey counts 30 legs when looking at the pigs and geese. How many pigs and geese might there be?

____ Pigs   ____ Geese

After we fed the horses we filled up their water containers. There were 3 big containers that were all different shapes. Funnily enough they all held the same amount of water.

6. What might the containers look like?

48

The horses' paddock was next to the cows' paddock. Pop said he would take us out for a ride on the horses tomorrow afternoon.

7. Bailey counts 25 animals in the paddocks. How many horses might there be and how many cows might there be?

As I wandered back into the house I heard the cuckoo clock go again. I think I'd heard it five times since I got up.

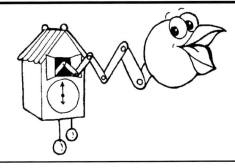

8. What time might it be now and what time might Bailey have got up?

Nan asked if I could set the table ready for lunch. I went and got a plate, a fork, a knife and a cup for each person.

9. How many pieces might be needed altogether?

After lunch we helped Nan make jam. Nan made the best jam in the world! She sells jars of it at the local market. This weekend we are going to help her. I wonder how many jars we will sell?

10. If Nan sells the jam for €2 a jar, how much money will she make?

As I was getting ready for bed later that night I heard Pop telling Justin there was a 30% chance of rain tomorrow. I hoped it wasn't going to rain because we had planned to go horse riding in the afternoon. What does *a 30% chance* mean? Do you think it will rain?

There is a 30% chance of rain tomorrow.

Ready-Ed Publications

Activity 1 - Temperature Differences

The temperature can be quite different across the seasons. Imagine if the temperature was different from one day to the next.

❑ Roll a 20-sided dice and record your first roll as the temperature for Day 1 and your second roll as the temperature for Day 2. Work out the difference between the two temperatures.

Day 1	Day 2	Difference

Questions

1. What is the greatest difference in temperature that you recorded?

_____

2. Which is the smallest difference in temperature that you recorded?

_____

Ready-Ed Publications

Activity 2 - Earning Money

❑ Bailey is trying to save up €30 for a new game. If Bailey does all her set chores around the house every day, her mum will give her €1 tomorrow and a Euro more every day after that. So she will receive €1 tomorrow, €2 the next day, €3 the day after that, and so on. If she saves all that money for 10 days will she have enough to buy the €30 game?

Prediction:

	Amount Given	Total
Day 1	€1	€1
Day 2		
Day 3		
Day 4		
Day 5		
Day 6		
Day 7		
Day 8		
Day 9		
Day 10		

Questions

1. Did Bailey earn enough money to buy her new game? How much money did she earn?

_____

2. After how many days does she have €30?

_____

3. How many days would it take her to earn €60?

_____

Ready-Ed Publications

Activity 3 - How Many Legs?

❏ On Farmer Jed's farm he has lots of horses, ducks and sheep. If we know there are 48 legs altogether on the farm, how many of each animal could there be? How many different combinations can you find?

Horses	Ducks	Sheep
2 (8 legs)	16 (32 legs)	2 (8 legs)

Questions

1. How many different combinations did you find?

   _____

2. How many different combinations do you think there might be?

   _____

3. How will you know when you have found all the possible combinations?

   _____

Ready-Ed
Publications

Section Six:
Transport

Ready-Ed
Publications

TRANSPORT

SUPPORT & EXTENSION QUESTIONS

1. If there are 24 wheels in a car park, how many vehicles might there be?
   Support: If the vehicles are all cars, how many vehicles might there be?
   Extension: Have you considered all vehicles? How many different combinations can you find?

2. How many wheels might this be?
   Support: If there are 9 motorbikes, how many wheels are there?
   Extension: What is the maximum number of wheels there could be? What is the minimum number of wheels there could be?

3. If there are 30 wheels at Jack's house, how many cars and motorbikes might he have?
   Support: If there are 9 motorbikes, how many cars are there?
   Extension: How will you know when you have found every possible combination?

4. What might this pattern look like?
   Support: If the cars are all red, black or white, what might the pattern look like?
   Extension: What if the number plates make a pattern? What might this look like?

5. What might this tally look like?
   Support: What if there are 20 cars and most are white?
   Extension: What car colour do you think would be recorded the most/least and why? Does your tally show this? Can you transform your tally into a graph?

6. Can you work out how many planes might fly over the school in one day?
   Support: What if there are 2 planes that fly over the school each hour?
   Extension: What would the peak time for flying be? How many planes might pass over the school within 24 hours? How might they be spread out over the day?

7. If there are 8 empty spaces in the car park, how many might be taken and how many spaces might there be altogether?
   Support: If only 13 spaces are taken, how many spaces are there altogether? What if there are only 2 empty spaces in the car park?
   Extension: What if half of the spaces are taken?

8. Can you think of some other ways that students might travel to school? Can you draw what the graph might look like?
   Support: What if there are 20 people in the class and 2 people travel by bus? Can you create a graph which includes this information?
   Extension: Think of other ways that students might get to school and make sure you record this on your graph.

TRANSPORT

SUPPORT & EXTENSION QUESTIONS

9. Can you draw a map showing the way that you get from your home to your school?
   Support: Draw your house and draw your school. Create a path from one to the other showing the turns that you make to get to school. Can you add in any other landmarks?
   Extension: Can you draw your map as a bird's eye view? Remember to include all landmarks.

10. Write a set of directions for a friend so they can get from your house to school.
    Support: Using the map that you created, write out the turns that you have drawn.
    Extension: Is there more than one route? Write an alternative set of directions.

Answers

Discussion (after) (Page 56)

Can you write down as many number plates as you can where the digits add up to make 10?
E.g. 451; 226; 712; 910
If there are 40 wheels, how many vehicles might there be?
E.g. 10 cars. 5 cars plus 10 motorbikes. 20 motorbikes. 8 cars plus 4 motorbikes.

Activity Pages
How Many Wheels? (Page 61)

(possible answers)

Bikes	Trikes	Wheels
0	12	36
1	11	35
2	10	34
12	0	24
11	1	25
10	2	26
9	3	27

24 Wheels (Page 62)

Vehicle	How many make 24 wheels?
cars	6
trikes	8
small truck (6 wheels)	4
motorbikes	12
large truck (8 wheels)	3

Discussion (before):

- ❑ How many different types of transport are there?
- ❑ How many different types of transport have you been on?
- ❑ What is the most/least amount of wheels a vehicle can have?
- ❑ How many wheels are at your house?
- ❑ How do you get to school and why?

Discussion (after):

- ❑ Can you write down as many number plates as you can where the digits add up to make 10?
- ❑ If there are 40 wheels, how many vehicles might there be?
- ❑ The vehicles in a car park make a pattern. Can you draw what this pattern might look like?
- ❑ Write a set of directions to get from one area in the school to another. Give them to a friend to follow. Did your friend make it to the right spot?

Ready-Ed Publications

A MATHS STORY: TRANSPORT

Read the story *Transport* and solve the problems along the way.

"Smash!" yelled Jack, crashing his car into mine. Jack loved cars, trains, buses, trucks, planes ... he loved all methods of transport! I remember when we were in Jack's mum's car parked at the shops and Jack turned to me and said, "Did you know there are 24 wheels in this carpark?" I didn't know if he was right, but I was impressed that he had even attempted to count them!

1. If there are 24 wheels in a car park, how many vehicles might there be?

Jack and I were playing at the car track, Jack's favourite place to play at school. A few others were playing there too. Between us all we had 9 vehicles.

2. How many wheels might this be?

Jack's whole family loved cars and motorbikes. One day I went for a play at Jack's house and it looked like there were cars and bikes everywhere. Even Jack had his own little motorbike. I could just imagine my Mum's face if I asked for a motorbike!

3. If there are 30 wheels at Jack's house, how many cars and motorbikes might he have?

As we were playing at the car track, Jack ran off to get a car that had rolled away and I looked up at the cars driving past the school. I watched a few cars go by and then a minute later another group go by. By the time 10 cars had passed I realised they made a pattern!

4. What might this pattern look like?

Once, our teacher, Mrs. Sander, had taken us out of school one day to collect some data on the colours of the cars that drove by. We had to create a tally for every red, blue, black and white car that we saw.

5. What might this tally look like?

red | blue | black | white

Jack came back and pointed out a plane flying over us. "That's the second one I have seen since we came out to play," he said. "And I noticed two at recess".

6. Can you work out how many planes might fly over the school in one day?

Ready-Ed Publications

Looking to the other side of the school we could see the teachers' car park. Normally it was full but I could see 8 empty spaces today. I wondered where everyone was.

7. If there are 8 empty spaces in the car park, how many might be taken and how many spaces might there be altogether?

The music started so we scooped up all the cars and ran to class. On the board Mrs. Sander had written, *Walk to School Day*.

"As it is *Walk to School Day* next Friday I thought we would find out how people in our class travel to school each day," she said. We shared some ways that we travelled to school, then we did a survey and Mrs. Sander made a table on the board. Half the class came by car, a quarter walked and there were others who travelled to school in other ways. Then we were asked to create a graph to show the results.

8. Can you think of some of the other ways that students might travel to school? Can you draw what the graph might look like?

During the next lesson we started talking about the directions that we take to get to school. Then Mrs. Sander asked us to draw a map showing the route we take from home to school. I closed my eyes and tried to picture the streets that we turned down and which way we turned.

9. Can you draw a map showing the way that you get from your home to your school?

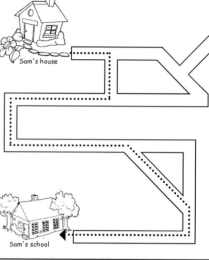

Sam's house

Sam's school

"That looks great Sam," said Mrs. Sander as she walked past. "Could you now use your map to write a set of directions that someone else could follow to get from your house to school?" I was sure that I could.

10. Write a set of directions for a friend so they can get from your house to school.

"Want to come to my house tomorrow and ride bikes?" Jack asked after school. "Sure," I smiled. "I'll ask my mum when I get home."

I thought as I walked to the car what Jack might be when he's older. There are heaps of jobs that involve all kinds of transport. Can you think of some jobs that he could do?

Ready-Ed
Publications

Activity 1 - How Many Wheels?

❑ There are many different types of vehicles and many of them have different amount of wheels. If there are 12 bicycles and tricycles in a shop window, can you work out how many of each there might be and how many wheels there might be?

Bikes	Trikes	Wheels
0	12	36

Activity 2 - 24 Wheels

❏ Jack counts 24 wheels in a car park. How many of each vehicle might this be?

Vehicle	How many make 24 wheels?
car	
trike	
small truck (6 wheels)	
motorbike	
large truck (8 wheels)	

❏ What if Jack counts 30 wheels? How many of each vehicle might this be?

Vehicle	How many make 30 wheels?
car	
trike	
small truck (6 wheels)	
motorbike	
large truck (8 wheels)	

Ready-Ed
Publications